AF365482

Published by the authors
2024
Strasbourg, France
ISBN 978-2-9595397-0-1

CLIMATE CHANGE IS A CLASS ISSUE

CLIMATE CHANGE IS A CLASS ISSUE

Not just because the one-per-cent produce most
carbon dioxide — though they do

Or because those at the bottom feel the effects
first — though that's true

Or because elites use their crisis as an excuse to
squeeze the rest — when won't they?

Or because countries that pollute the least will
suffer the worst — when don't they?

But because the system that exploits the planet to
destruction is the same that depends on class
exploitation: the system that sees everything in
terms of profit — which is what capitalism is

While the changes needed to bring our world back
from the precipice are the same that would end this
class exploitation: an economy of the people by the
people and for the people — which is what socialism
should be

And what can make this happen if not the combined
power of the working class?

CLIMATE CHANGE IS A CLASS ISSUE

Sarah Glynn

John Clarke

66 This is a small book but its message is vital.
Those who exploit the labour of others
for profit also exploit the earth's precious
resources for the same reason. If you
campaign to save the planet, join a picket
line, and vice versa. The struggle doesn't
change – it is the class struggle, and this time
we must win. Thank you Sarah and John. 99

KEN LOACH

CONTENTS

"Climate change
has placed all
humankind before a
great choice: to
continue in the ways of
capitalism and death,
or to start down the path
of harmony with nature
and respect for life."

Evo Morales

CLIMATE CHANGE IS A CLASS ISSUE

In the end, climate change impacts everyone. It will even get those who are raking in fortunes by destroying the planet: people who can buy their way out of temporary discomforts. It impacts the whole of the natural world. So why claim it is a class issue? This little book sets out to answer that question. It also looks at why this matters, and what this means we can do to avert the threat that hangs over us all.

Climate change is our biggest and most imminent danger, but our world crisis goes beyond even that. By treating the planet as a limitless resource, our modern society is destroying the environment everywhere. That is a class issue too, and part of this discussion.

We begin with what we can see around us.

Not just because the one-per-cent produce most carbon dioxide – though they do

We know that carbon dioxide in the air allows light from the sun to pass through, but traps the heat given out by the warmed earth. Already in the nineteenth century, people were beginning to recognise that increases in carbon dioxide produced by the industrial revolution could increase the heat trapped and make our planet warmer.

Carbon dioxide is produced when we burn fuel to heat our homes or drive cars or fly planes. It is also produced when energy is used to make and transport things. Even things that are sold as energy savers may have already used a lot of energy and produced a lot of carbon dioxide in their manufacture.

Most of the things we buy are also made from materials that will be only partly recycled. They will be thrown away as though those materials are replaceable, but we can't go on doing that for ever. We can't go on burying and burning billions of dustbins full of stuff every week.

Wealthier people have bigger homes and more cars. They go on more flights and have more possessions and throw away more things. Their wealth is based on businesses and investments that produce carbon dioxide and boost consumerism. The wealthier people are, the more carbon dioxide they tend to produce, the more resources they use, the more they are invested in fossil fuels - and the more they contribute to the environmental crisis.

Or because those at the bottom feel the effects first – though that's true

The crisis will catch up with the wealthy too in the end, but for now they can buy themselves some protection. They can afford homes away from the most dangerous flood plains and install energy-consuming cooling systems. They can choose not to work in extreme heat. When weather changes reduce supplies of foods, they can pay extra to make sure that they still get what they want. The poorer people are, the more likely they are to suffer serious consequences in times of disaster or be priced out of essential supplies in times of scarcity.

Or because elites use their crisis as an excuse to squeeze the rest – when won't they?

On top of this, those in power are using the crisis to further exploit the people who are least responsible for causing it; just like they used the economic crash of 2008. They demand sacrifices by those with least to give. In Western countries, the politics of the last forty-five years has been aimed at reversing the gains made by workers in the decades following the second world war. It has been aimed at ensuring that most of the wealth that is created benefits those who are already wealthy; that hard-won services are sold off to private companies who will exploit their users; and that the ability to protest these things becomes more and more limited. Western powers have used their economic dominance to force similar policies on the Global South. Every disaster has been used as an opportunity for the wealthy to take back more of the world's resources, and environmental collapse is no exception.

Always, there is pressure to preserve existing hierarchies and to extract more from working people. Politicians claim that they can combat climate change without disturbing the way our existing society functions. Their policies often end up penalising the less well-off while having little impact on carbon dioxide production. Some even cause production to increase.

Policy makers say that they can persuade people to produce less carbon dioxide by using taxes to raise energy costs. But wealthy people, who are the biggest producers, can afford to pay more, and the energy savings achieved are very far from what is needed. Meanwhile, the rise in costs affects everyone and may make the difference between a lower-income family just managing and that family spiralling into debt. In France, increased fuel duty, introduced as a 'green policy', triggered massive popular demonstrations in the movement that became known as the *gilets jaunes*, after the yellow vests worn by the protestors.

Rather than approach the introduction of energy saving systems logically and efficiently, this politics treats them as another business opportunity. Subsidies for green home improvements have fed the shareholders of a new generation of private companies. Where the companies have been properly regulated, they have also benefitted homeowners, but renters continue to pay the extra costs of living in energy inefficient homes.

Failure to meet modern insulation standards has been used as an excuse to demolish social housing and sell the land to private developers, although demolition and rebuilding is a hugely energy intensive process.

The working class is the least responsible for the environmental catastrophe and the most badly affected, and so-called environmental policies often increase inequality. Policies that make life more difficult for the working class are rightly protested. But environmental policies do not have to be like this: quite the opposite in fact.

Or because countries that pollute the least will suffer the worst – when don't they?

Similar things are happening on an international scale. Rich 'developed' countries have already produced way more than their fair share of carbon dioxide; while poor ex-colonial countries are often least protected from rising sea levels and the extreme weather conditions that climate change is making more and more common. Decades of pillage, together with privatisations imposed by the World Bank, have left them without the infrastructure needed for everyday life, let alone for coping with mass disaster.

These poorer countries have long been exploited for their resources by richer countries and multinationals. Climate change brings new opportunities for exploitation. It brings new demands for rare minerals to feed new green technologies (such as lithium for batteries), and it brings pressure from businesses in richer countries that want to relocate their polluting industries. Those richer countries can then appear to meet their green targets, and the businesses can avoid strict environmental regulations.

Within poorer countries, it is, again, those with least who are most exposed to the impacts of climate change, and to the exploitation carried out in the name of combatting it.

But because the system that exploits the planet to destruction is the same that depends on class exploitation: the system that sees everything in terms of profit – which is what capitalism is

The reason for the mismatch between responsibility and suffering is the same for climate change and the wider environmental crisis as it is for all aspects of the world's increasing and brutal inequality. It is the result of capitalism: of capitalism's prioritisation of profit and its need for constant economic growth. Market competition means that no business can afford to be content with what it has, as it risks being overtaken by its competitors. It must find new markets and create new demand. It must persuade us to buy products and services we neither need nor truly want, at the

"What the climate
needs to avoid collapse
is a contraction in
humanity's use of resources;
what our economic model demands
to avoid collapse is unfettered
expansion. Only one of these sets
of rules can be changed, and it's
not the laws of nature."

Naomi Klein

"In a consumer society,
contentment is a radical proposition.
Recognizing abundance rather than scarcity
undermines an economy that thrives by
creating unmet desires."

Robin Wall Kimmerer

expense of more and more of the world's resources. Everything is regarded as a potential source of profit. Capitalism exploits nature in the same way that capitalism exploits the working class. How both are treated depends only on their potential to make money.

When everything is left to the market, that is to private businesses, the economy doesn't work in the service of society. Rather, society works for the economy; and that economy is locked into rapacious world-devouring expansion. If we were asked to invent a system for meeting human needs, we would, rightly, be suspicious of any proposal that put the priority not on need but on private profit. And we would outright reject any proposal that depended on limitless consumption of our limited common inheritance.

Meanwhile, capitalism's constant need for more raw materials and more markets helps to drive countries towards war – when the working class is used as cannon fodder, and the environment is regarded as equally dispensable.

The manmade rules of the capitalist system are generally referred to as though they were unchangeable laws of nature: as though we had no choice but to organise society to put profit before everything. We might think it would be better to focus on human need and well-being and on living in tune with our natural environment, but we are told that that is not how the world works. We are told that people are innately selfish and that it is only through selfish competition that society develops. However, if we were really the selfish creatures the economists depict, human society would never have got off the ground. Humanity's strength comes from our ability to organise together and help each other. We are told that planning for any form of society other than a capitalist one is not realistic – as though continuing with a system that is making our planet unliveable is a 'realistic' thing to do.

While the changes needed to bring our world back from the precipice are the same that would end this class exploitation: an economy of the people by the people and for the people – which is what socialism should be

The absurd thing is that we know that it is perfectly possible for humanity to live – and live well – without this costing the earth. We know the changes that need to be made in the way our society is organised, and we know how to use public funding to provide public goods and services and genuinely useful work. We know that if resources are shared equally and used rationally there is enough for everyone.

The changes required are big, but they are necessary for survival. They can also bring about a much happier and less stressful way of living. However, these changes threaten existing hierarchies, and are resisted by those in power.

One way that elites persuade the rest of us to support their interests – their very short-term interests in this case – is to make us fearful of change. We are told that we will lose our freedom and our way of life. We are not supposed to question what freedoms are threatened – the freedom to make the world uninhabitable, for example, or the freedom to exploit others. Nor are we expected to ask if a way of life that generates massive inequality and that sees most people spend most of their waking hours tied to tedious and insecure labour is a way of life that should be preserved unchanged.

Many of the things we value most – being with family and

friends, making and enjoying music or art, dancing, playing and watching sport, exploring the natural world that surrounds us – do not need to use large amounts of valuable energy, nor to use up irreplaceable and limited resources. But we are always restricted in our enjoyment of these things because we are forced to spend so much of our lives on the capitalist treadmill. We use energy and resources to make more and more stuff that adds very little to human wellbeing, and we use our ingenuity to persuade others that this stuff is the key to their future happiness. This is what the capitalist system requires of us. We must never be happy with what we have, or we wouldn't buy more. We work long hours, often on jobs that we can perceive are intrinsically pointless, and then spend our hard-won earnings on things that might save us a bit of time or seem to replace a bit of lost joy. We are caught on a treadmill that is designed to deprive us of both the time and the inclination to think beyond capitalist expectations.

Most jobs do not contribute much to humanity, but workers doing those jobs are dependent on them for a living. They can't afford to see their livelihood disappear. Capitalists exploit the fear of unemployment like they always do. They use this fear to make people resistant to any change that would see these jobs go. However, a sustainable social system requires work too, just different work. Such a system can pay people to do the work that their community decides is important, and it can ensure, through a fairer distribution of resources, that everyone has enough to live on and enough time to enjoy life.

Public ownership of resources becomes even more important with the growth of AI. AI has the potential for generating big savings in the amount of human labour needed to sustain societies. In public hands, it can enable everyone to benefit. If left to capitalist markets, it will only produce greater inequality.

Public investment in alternative energy can ensure that this is developed in a way that best benefits society, rather than for maximum private profit.

Capitalism also teaches us to believe that endless economic growth is essential for our well-being. Only when we look out from behind the capitalist blinkers, can we see a clear route off this pathway to destruction. If public and communal organisations, at all levels, can provide for our basic needs, then we no longer have to rely on the market, with its insatiable appetite.

On every occasion when we demand public expenditure for the public good, we are told that the money isn't available. At the same time, we are surrounded by wealth – by the products of generations of labour – and we have new technologies that allow labour to achieve ever greater productivity. If only there was a way to direct that wealth to where it is most needed… But, of course, there is.

Governments – national and regional – have the tools: it's just that capitalism demands that they don't use them. Public authorities at all levels have the ability to invest in changes that enable a more sustainable way of living – things such as affordable and comprehensive public transport. They can do this in a similar way to how Britain's war-battered economy built the national health service. And governments can design taxation systems that prevent wealth being horded by the rich and allow it to be used to benefit everyone. Wealth taxes as well as income taxes can access wealth that has been built up in the past, as well as wealth being created today.

When public authorities invest in this way, money doesn't just disappear, it is used to build our shared wealth. This can provide a source of revenue for more public investment, or it can enable the provision of public goods and services. Free or subsidised goods and services contribute towards a more equal society. They can take us a step closer to a more needs-based community-centred economy.

We have been conditioned by capitalism to reject higher taxes and public spending, but if we want a rational world, with democratic control over the economy, these are vital tools.

This is not an argument for returning to centralised insensitive bureaucracies, such as dominated Eastern Europe or managed the public housing programmes of post-war social democracy. Democratic control demands that people have the opportunity to get involved in running their lives and in making the decisions that affect them. It means making decisions at the most local level possible.

Capitalism has persuaded us that public ownership and control should be a temporary last resort when a part of the capitalist economy has failed. But, if we want a sustainable and fair use of resources, a publicly owned and run economy should be our aim. This would not affect small businesses, just vital services and big enterprises that have come to dictate our economy and are sacrificing the future of humanity for their short-term profit.

Business owners will protest that public investment provides unfair competition, making their business less profitable. If those businesses are providing a needed role and can't survive, they too can be taken into public ownership and control. The loss in private-sector jobs could be more than compensated by secure public-sector jobs.

The success of anti-change propaganda has allowed the 'pragmatists' to declare social change impossible due to lack of public support. Instead, they claim that all that is needed to stop climate change is a technological fix. New technologies have an important role. Wind, solar power, and heat pumps can all make a vital contribution to reducing carbon emissions; but, on their own, new technologies focused on green energy will not be enough. They will not prevent the ever-expanding consumption of the worlds resources; and some consume even more resources themselves, including rare metals. Some technologies risk generating new, potentially huge, unknown problems. And, without societal change, every increase in renewable energy tends to be used to justify greater energy use.

If a fraction of the effort spent chasing the mirage of cure-all technology was redirected to reorganising society, our future prospects would be much brighter. While politicians and business people look to technology to save capitalism, scientists are increasingly recognising that it is only by ending capitalism that humanity can save itself.

And what can make this happen if not the combined power of the working class?

When the working class acts together, that creates the power to take on the vested interests that are sending us all to hell in a handcart. In fact, this is our only hope.

The gains of the past were not the products of elite generosity. They were won after long campaigns in which people united so that they were impossible to resist.

In this struggle for the survival of humanity, we have seen brave resistance by indigenous peoples whose existence has been threatened, we have seen climate scientists discarding the muzzle of political 'neutrality', and we have seen millions of schoolchildren demand a future; but without the working class, this struggle for survival lacks the weight and the power to make a difference.

Survival demands revolutionary change to the economy, and the backbone of the economy is its workers. When workers take action together, including planned and strategic withdrawal of their labour, they have the power to make continuation with existing practices impossible: the power to force change. They also have knowledge and skills that can be turned towards creating a different way of doing things.

Four decades of neoliberalism have narrowed the horizons of organised labour. Unions are hemmed in by legislation, and union leaders have internalised restrictions on moving beyond immediate issues in the individual workplace; but the situation can change, as it has been made to do in the past. The urgency of our current predicament should fuel the forces of change, which will not come from sleep-inducing mission statements but from the pressure of workers en masse. The power of organised labour can force changes from both industry and government.

Outwith the workplace, too, when working-class communities

come together, they can rescue aspects of their lives from the capitalist juggernaut and demonstrate, on a community-scale, that other, better, approaches to social organisation are possible.

"GDP
growth is,
ultimately, an
indicator of
the welfare of
capitalism. That
we have all come to see it
as a proxy for the welfare
of humans represents an
extraordinary ideological coup"

Jason Hickel

"We'll go down
in history as the first
society that wouldn't save
itself because it wasn't
cost-effective."

attrib Donella H. Meadows
or Kurt Vonnegut

A MANIFESTO FOR CHANGE

If human society is to survive, it will have to undergo many changes. The existential threat facing our planet demands a complete change in the way society is organised and run; but capitalism has been much too successful in normalising a capitalist mindset for that to happen easily. For very many people, capitalism is seen simply as the natural order of things, and they are ready to agree with the capitalist elite that any action that is seen as threatening capitalism should be opposed.

There is not yet popular support for all the changes that are needed. We can, though, enact and campaign for changes now that are both beneficial in themselves and that can help people see the necessity and possibility of more radical change – change that breaks the shackles of capitalism.

This 'manifesto' will not attempt to give a detailed programme – though it will suggest examples of changes that could provide the focus of campaigns and action. Its purpose is to set out an overriding framework, based on the arguments in the previous section. This framework should inform campaigning decisions and actions in such a way that many small changes trigger much larger ones, and that people come to realise how capitalism has blinded them to their real interests.

Public need not private greed

Inequality, and capitalism's dependence on private businesses to meet basic needs, have enabled a relatively small number of people to exploit both the rest of the population and our shared natural resources. As the previous section argued, the survival of human society demands a new sort of economics. Competition and the drive for endless growth needs to be replaced by prioritisation of human need, including the needs of future generations. The exploitation of both people and nature needs to be replaced by an understanding of human society as part of a natural ecosystem that has to be nurtured.

Our limited resources need to be shared more equally and used more rationally. This can be achieved by using public funding to provide public goods and services and genuinely useful work; and by using taxes to reduce inequalities and allow everyone to benefit from efficiencies of production and from the wealth built up by past generations.

At the same time, local communities can put these principles into practice now through mutual aid organisations. These can help with daily life, and also provide a living model of a different way of approaching the economy, and of inclusive democratic structures.

From neighbourhood co-ops to campaigns to force change in government policy, actions guided by these principles can both move societies onto a more environmentally sustainable path and bring a better quality of life. They can expose the lies of those who argue that escaping capitalism is impossible and that green politics equates to deprivation. Every positive improvement won boosts demands for further change.

History shows that this scenario is not simply wishful thinking. Even devotees of minimal public intervention accept the need to move beyond a capitalist free-for-all in many areas of life. They accept the need for restrictions on what people can do – such as planning laws – and they take many public services for granted – such as schools and roads and sewage systems and street lighting and pensions and (in many places) healthcare. These services were won through historical struggles and through the political necessity of basic standards of health and literacy. Today, our very survival demands that public intervention is extended much further.

More services at both national and local levels can be run in
the interests of local communities rather than for profit. Public
healthcare is not only more equitable but also more cost
effective. Subsidised, or even free, public transport can change
the liveability of a city and make it accessible for everyone.
Subsidised public housing can be integrated with wider planning
and prevent housing being used for speculation and exploitation.

In the past, public ownership suffered from distant and
insensitive centralised bureaucracies, but it needn't be this
way. With democratic control by workers and users, and with
local management, public services can respond to real needs.
Our lives and our planet require us to maximise democratic
engagement, and that means organising things at the most local
level possible. Politicians like to talk about devolution, meaning
the state handing down power from above, but in a democracy,
power should come from the people. Our campaigns should be
aimed at a democratic model that builds up from the bottom, with
each level of organisation working within its region and coming
together with others to address bigger shared concerns.

Looking beyond the traditional realms of the public economy,
public investment in AI and in new technologies can allow these
to be put to use for the benefit of everyone, and not just to provide

riches for a few while many others are put out of work. And any serious response to climate change must include public energy companies dedicated to building up green energy generation. These can site generating centres where they work best (not according to the profits of private landowners) and deliver energy where it is needed.

This list is far from comprehensive.

Increased public involvement in the economy would also allow everyone to be given a guarantee of a job doing socially useful work at a decent wage and with decent conditions. And decent conditions should include short working hours so people have more time to spend as they will, and more time to get involved in running their community.

Public services can be economically efficient and can increase public wealth, but if they are to be free or subsidised for users, then costs need to be recovered through taxation. Those with a lot of money to lose have been very effective in persuading others that taxes are detrimental for everyone and must be resisted. However, taxes can be targeted on those most able to pay. Besides higher rates of income tax for those with large incomes, top rates can be increased for taxes on inheritance and gifts, and much more use can be made of wealth taxes, including land value tax.

"It's hard
to imagine a
surer sign that one
is dealing with an
irrational economic system
than the fact that the
prospect of eliminating
drudgery is considered to be
a problem."

David Graeber

"Environmentalism without
class struggle is
gardening"

Chico Mendes

Taxation can reduce the wealth gap while bringing in money that can be used efficiently for the benefit of all. A system that employs progressive taxation, in which the wealthy are taxed a greater proportion of their income and wealth, and that uses those taxes to fund public goods and services, is a system that benefits the great majority of people. Besides the immediate benefits, more equal societies have been shown to be better for everyone on a whole range of criteria. And if this economic shift can keep this planet habitable, it becomes vital for the whole of humanity.

Legal restrictions not costly bribes

Taxes and subsidies have also been used to try and encourage or disincentivise certain behaviours, such as subsidies to help energy-guzzling businesses to change their product or their production methods, or taxes that penalise waste and pollution. However, tax and subsidies used in this way can prove a clumsy tool with unintended consequences. Subsidies, if not carefully delineated, can largely end up boosting corporate profits. Taxes to change behaviour need to be precisely targeted, else they will only penalise those least able to pay, leaving the main offenders to continue with their former practices. Many big users of energy and other resources can easily swallow the extra cost – or, in the case of businesses, pass it on to their customers. These types of policy waste public funds and distract from pursuing more effective methods. Badly thought through 'solutions' also make people question climate change policies as a whole.

If activities are ecologically destructive, they need to be banned outright. Bans should close down polluting industries, stop the opening of new oil and gas fields, and increasingly restrict drilling of existing fields. Such bans need to be accompanied by public development of alternative energy generation, as well as by reductions in energy use. With public investment and a job guarantee, industries can be closed without leaving people out of work. Instead of working in industries that damage the planet, they can be guaranteed work that benefits their community.

Other laws can help temper capitalism's demands. Inequality could be reduced with a legal cap on the difference between the highest and lowest wages within an organisation. Businesses could be required to make their products easier to repair, and to give longer guarantees so as to reduce planned obsolescence. The constant pressure for consumption could be eased by banning advertising from public space.

Focusing the power of organised labour

For these changes to happen will require committed and strategic mass campaigning. The working class has the power to force change because of its size and because of its vital role in keeping our economic and social structures afloat. Workers can also help ensure that actions target key points in those structures, and use their skills to devise greener ways of working.

Trade unions enable workers to use their power as workers to force change.[1] Workers are not victims needing protection, as portrayed in some writing about the 'green transition'. They are subjects who can and must play a proactive role in building a genuinely sustainable future. They can use their combined power to push industries towards green alternatives, and to demand public involvement at all levels – state, municipal, and neighbourhood. This is not just about preserving jobs when old polluting industries close down, or ensuring that businesses don't use the transition to replace secure work with a gig-economy. It is about taking the initiative, so that changes made are not a greenwash conceived in the interest of shareholders, but are guided by the interests of wider society – indeed of humanity.

Building up our trade unions must be a vital part of any ecological strategy, including fighting for the secure jobs that give trade unions their strength. Unions will need to confront the legal restrictions constraining their actions. They can link environmental

demands to employment issues where this is possible, but will
have to be ready to challenge those restrictions when this is not
enough.

A manifesto for trade unions needs to take the long view, looking
at the future of work and workers, and beyond immediate
difficulties. And it must encompass a wide geography, bringing
together workers across the world to facilitate strategic and
coordinated actions that can force change on our globally linked
economy.

Community activism as a force for change

So far, I have talked about campaigns to force others to act – to
put irresistible pressure on government or local authorities or
on employers – but some changes can be instigated by local
communities themselves.

When communities work together to pool and share resources
and skills, this doesn't need official involvement or endorsement.
Mutual aid organisations can enable sharing of resources,
with initiatives such as tool libraries, carpools, and all sorts of
shared neighbourhood amenities. These can also serve to bring
local people together, facilitating other forms of mutual aid and

"Practicing
mutual aid is the
surest means for
giving each other and to
all the greatest safety,
the best guarantee of
existence and progress,
bodily, intellectual
and moral."

Pyotr Kropotkin

"The economy
regains its true
meaning as an area of
social action."

Abdullah Öcalan

solidarity. In community gardens, for example, people work together, organise together, and learn from one another, and can chose how to distribute the produce.[2] They can pass knowledge and tools and very literal seed funding to other similar groups.

For those who don't enjoy getting their hands dirty, mutual aid communities involve many different aspects of life, including developers of open-source software.

Mutual aid principles can be extended to provide livelihoods and housing through workers' co-ops and housing co-ops. They can also form the basis of responsive local management of public resources, as in Glasgow's tenant management co-ops (which disappeared when the council transfered all its housing stock to the market-led Glasgow Housing Association). In a capitalist economy, this sort of organisation requires especial dedication and hard work. It also requires compromises to access initial funding or to work with the authorities, but each successful example makes it easier for others.

Community organisations of all kinds already provide the cement that holds our societies together, and local achievements can provide inspiration and support for more and bigger changes. But national and local authorities, which rarely acknowledge the vital

role such organisations play, restrict the possibility for these to
have a wider impact by promoting the idea that they should not
be 'political'. With formal politics having acquired such a bad
name, this can seem superficially alluring. Official authorities can
actively support community organisation, but they can also stifle
its potential through institutionalisation and shutting down critical
voices – as so many community activists have discovered.

If they can escape the pressure to keep out of 'politics', and avoid
being treated as a sticking plaster for the wounds of capitalism,
community activists and organisations can develop grass roots
democratic engagement and provide a strong force for wider
progressive change.

Granby Four Streets in Liverpool demonstrates the potential, and
also the hard graft and conviviality, of community organising.[3]
As in many other examples of mutual aid, the Granby residents
were responding to an external threat – in this case the
planned demolition of their homes. Liverpool City Council was
demolishing hundreds of terraced houses to make room for
speculative development – and they were encouraging decline
to force residents to sell. In Granby Four Streets, people not
only refused to leave, they set about demonstrating that this
was a place that should not be demolished. They turned the

neighbourhood into a green oasis, painted the tinned up empty homes, and set up a regular street market. Granby was just one of the areas fighting demolition, and, aided by changed economic conditions and by the conservation lobby, campaigners got the demolitions stopped in time to save the Granby homes. The nearby Welsh Streets were saved too, but too late for the community that had lived in them. In Granby, residents stepped into the gap and established a community land trust to renovate empty homes for local people, including turning two of the houses into a winter garden and community arts centre. Whenever large sums of money are involved, compromises are inevitable. Some of the renovated homes are rented at below market rates, but others have had to be sold; and the need to raise funds will inevitably restrict potential for involvement in wider politics. However, land trust members try to involve neighbouring areas, and to spread knowledge of what is possible.

Real life doesn't separate what happens in the workplace from what happens outside, and campaigns multiply their strength when they combine trade union and community organisation. A demonstration of this in action is provided by the former GKN auto-parts factory in Florence, where the union is organised under a factory collective.[4] What began, in July 2021, as a factory occupation against threatened closure and the lay-off of over 400 workers, has developed into a mass movement that brings together different struggles for a better way of living in society. Together with academic researchers and political activists, factory workers have compiled a plan for a green reindustrialisation from below. This would see their factory operating as a not-for-profit workers' cooperative making cargo bikes and solar panels and acting as a precedent for other workplaces. Even if they don't ultimately succeed in saving their factory – which would require external financial help – the workers are manufacturing a new politics.

This little book has been written for activists in so-called 'developed' economies, but some of the most powerful grassroots activism has been undertaken by indigenous communities outside those economies. These communities are resisting capitalist colonialism and oppression, which rides roughshod over environmentally harmonious traditional practices and communal land rights, and regards indigenous peoples and their lands as opportunities for mineral extraction, cheap labour, and the export of polluting industries. The capitalist forces that are threatening indigenous land and lives are the same as those exploiting workers and the natural world in the heart of 'developed' economies. Solidarity and coordination between struggles in both places make both stronger.

From small changes to new understandings

Each change achieved – through forcing new legislation or by direct community action – may seem very small compared to the enormity of what is needed, but one change can also make the next change easier. Together they can be greater than the sum of their parts and open our eyes to new possibilities.

Take public transport, for example. Every route won feeds into other potential routes and makes these more useful, and their construction easier to justify. Together, different routes can build up an efficient and practical network that all can use. There will always be some journeys and circumstances where individual cars are required – though these cars need not necessarily be individually owned – but when a public transport system is comprehensive, well-planned, and affordable, the majority of urban journeys can be made comfortably without a car. This makes possible a qualitative change in the nature of the city. The motor industry has conditioned us to regard the individual car as the symbol of success and freedom, but, when there is a practical alternative that means that many people are no longer dependent on cars for most journeys, we can see how cars have been allowed to dictate the nature of our environment. A society's reliance on cars actually deprives its citizens of choice. Even electric cars consume energy and resources, take up space, and contribute to hours spent stuck in traffic. With fewer cars, there is a lot more room for the things that make a city a pleasant place to live – including more trees and green spaces that can help to mitigate the impact of rising temperatures.

Every change that is carried out can help persuade more people of the viability of an approach that prioritises the inseparable wellbeing of humanity and of nature. So every change can make the next change easier. Developments on the ground can change people's outlook more quickly than theoretical debate. Examples of inclusive democratic practice and mutual aid are more convincing than essays, and every well-planned public investment demonstrates the hollowness of capitalist scare-stories.

Resisting elite reaction and imperialist war

Understandings may change more quickly than we might once have thought possible. History is moving at an astonishing speed, and many people are being forced to reassess their assumptions about world politics and government priorities. This is not a linear process – it is not just climate change that has tipping points. However, there is no guarantee that people's understandings will change in a positive direction.

The powerful react to crisis not by changing the actions that caused the crisis, but by clamping down on protest. Almost everywhere, political freedoms are being restricted and racisms are being encouraged so as to enable the old trick of divide and rule. When the already existing crises get overtaken by the even bigger crises resulting from climate change, governments will tend to reach for even more authoritarian solutions; and they will try and tame resistance through new versions of fascism.

Our defence against fascism is the struggle for real positive change, so that people are not lured by false promises. Such change must include a genuine inclusive democracy that responds to community needs. Campaigns for genuine democracy, with decisions taken as close to where they will be implemented as possible, have to be an integral part of any manifesto for change, with democratic practice beginning in campaigning organisations themselves.

Today, instead of focussing on the existential dangers of climate change and environmental exploitation, world politics is engulfed in growing conflict. Capitalist imperialism is generating a destructive competition between power blocks. Horrendous and terrifying in itself, this is making division when we most need cooperation, diverting attention from the failure to address environmental emergencies, and producing untold environmental damage. Peace is essential for a sustainable future, just as a sustainable future is essential for peace.

REFERENCES

1. ier.org.uk/wp-content/uploads/A5-web-PDF-IER_A5_Climate_v3_Nov23_2.pdf
2. freedomnews.org.uk/2024/05/14/growing-communities-in-waltham-forest
3. granby4streetsclt.co.uk; cooperativecity.org/2017/10/25/granby-four-streets-clt
4. facebook.com/coordinamentogknfirenze; labouroutlook.org/2024/06/25/gkn-workers-initiate-hunger-strike-for-worker%E2%80%91led-transition-in-europes-pivotal-struggle

"We
do not
need better
environmental policy
ideas to solve climate
change; *we need a
stronger working class.*
As long as we are losing
the larger class struggle,
we are also losing the
climate struggle."

*Matthew T.
Huber*

"The
plundering
of the human spirit by the
market place is paralleled by
the plundering of the earth by
capital."

Murray Bookchin

CLIMATE AND CLASS STRUGGLE

When the term 'class struggle' is used, we often think of strikes for better wages and improved working conditions or perhaps mass protests on the streets challenging social cutbacks. However, I'm going to argue that the rapidly developing climate disaster has everything to do with the class struggle and, indeed, will have the most profound impact on what working-class people must fight for and the nature of their struggles.

First of all, it is already abundantly clear that, just like the spread of the Covid pandemic, the impacts of climate change will play out along fault lines of social, racial, and global inequality. Even in wealthy countries, the destruction and devastation caused by extreme weather, wildfires, rising sea levels, and other climate effects will threaten people and communities who have the fewest resources and the most limited options to a much greater degree. In the Global South in particular, it is already horribly clear that the results of climate change mean catastrophic suffering.

As climate impacts intensify, those who face the worst consequences and who are being abandoned in the face of them will have to struggle to survive. They will have to advance demands and develop strategies and forms of organisation to confront those with economic and political power. The climate issue will be placed at the heart of the class struggle in country after country.

Assault on the natural world

Climate change and the broader environmental crisis are unfolding in a world that is dominated by capitalism and this deeply impacts how we must respond. A just and rational society would take urgent measures to curtail carbon emissions and transition to sustainable forms of economic activity. It would also, in a spirit of co-operation and solidarity, take the measures that were deemed necessary to minimise the impacts on the global population. Neither of these responses can be expected under the present system.

In his *Capitalism in the Anthropocene: Ecological Ruin or Ecological Revolution*, John Bellamy Foster argues that capitalism's competitive drive to generate profits and accumulate is at odds with creating a viable relationship with the natural world. He suggests that we face an 'irrational system of artificially stimulated growth, economic waste, financialized wealth, and extreme inequality' that threatens our existence.[1]

The evidence to support such a view is wide ranging and abundant. The escalating impacts of the climate crisis are to be found in the greatly increased levels of extreme heat, devastating droughts, violent storms, wildfires, and floods. However, the appalling failure to act in the face of these catastrophic impacts is an even more compelling reason to draw anti-capitalist conclusions.

In June 2024, *the Guardian* reported that 'the world's consumption of fossil fuels climbed to a record high last year, driving emissions to more than 40 gigatonnes of CO_2 for the first time, according to a global energy report.'[2] There is, moreover, nothing at all accidental about such a terrible development. Shell's CEO Wael Sawan, responding to a question about renewable energy sources, was very forthright when he stated, 'We will drive for strong returns in any business we go into... Our shareholders deserve to see us going after strong returns... Absolutely, we want to continue to go for lower and lower and lower carbon but it has to be profitable.'[3]

The conclusion that fundamental social change is needed is absolutely vital, but we must also ask ourselves how we can organise to make a difference in this society at the present dangerous moment. Foster's book puts forward the notion of an initial 'ecodemocratic phase' in the struggle that would 'demand a world of sustainable human development.' This would then go over to a 'more decisive, ecosocialist phase of the revolutionary struggle'.[4] Taking this perspective as a starting point, we can consider how we might organise and what our goals might be as the scale and intensity of the climate disaster intensifies.

The first and obvious consideration is to do all we can to stay the destructive hand of fossil fuel companies, banks, and other capitalist interests that have set us on the present path to environmental catastrophe. We must develop and apply the forms of mass action that can lead to the curtailing of emissions and the transition to renewable energy sources. In this regard, we are hardly starting from nowhere because a vital struggle for climate justice is already well and truly underway.

Climate movements have held mass rallies and organised ongoing campaigns to press their demands, and they have forced governments onto the defensive. There have also been more militant actions to actively disrupt the workings of fossil fuel companies and those who finance and enable them. This emerging wave of social resistance is global in its dimensions, and

"Would-be
green capitalism
is nothing but a
publicity stunt, a
label for the purpose
of selling a commodity,
or - in the best of cases
- a local initiative
equivalent to a
drop of water
on the arid soil
of the capitalist
desert."

Michael Löwy

"We live in
capitalism.
Its power
seems
inescapable.
So did the divine
right of kings.

Ursula K. Le Guin

we can only expect that the dire nature of the climate crisis will continue to drive this struggle.

Finding the way forward for the climate movement will involve a great deal of discussion, debate, and experimentation, in order to develop effective strategies. However, a basic point of agreement that I would argue is essential is that capitalist interests and political power structures must be faced with mass resistance and determined challenges if they are to be forced to make concessions. Those who think that they can win meaningful change by dialoguing with political leaders and fossil fuel lobbyists at climate summits are sadly mistaken. The United Nations Conference of Parties (COP) gatherings are a diversionary hoax that needs to be exposed and challenged for what it is.[5]

Climate impacts

As the effects of climate change become ever more extreme, which is now happening with unanticipated and alarming speed, it becomes starkly obvious that we are in nothing less than a struggle for survival. It is clear that many of the severe consequences that flow from climate change are now unavoidable. Populations are already being exposed to dire climate impacts and, even if we could make the transition to responsible environmental stewardship today, they are still going to get very much worse.

We may reasonably conclude that a social and economic system that wilfully compounds a planetary climate disaster is unlikely to place any more emphasis on keeping the mass of people safe in the face of that disaster than it is compelled to do. All that lies between us and social abandonment is our ability to challenge those in power with sufficient strength and determination to ensure our demands are met.

Working-class people will increasingly be faced with very major climate impacts in their workplaces and in the communities they are part of. The impacts of climate change are already a vital and pressing workers' issue. Justice for Migrant Workers (J4MW), which organises migrant farm workers in Ontario, Canada, is demanding that the government of that province 'implement emergency measures to protect farmworkers from extreme heat.' J4MW notes that 'farm workers are also 35 times more likely than the rest of the population to die of heat exposure.'[6]

In New York City, delivery drivers are challenging gig economy employers over their repeated exposure to heat as they go about their jobs,[7] and there are many such examples in a range of countries. In fact, the International Labour Organisation (ILO) suggests that 'more than 2.4 billion workers (out of a global workforce of 3.4 billion) are likely to be exposed to excessive heat at some point during their work.'[8]

In this dire situation, employers and governments are already trying to ensure that vital protections are denied to the greatest degree possible. In April 2024, Ron DeSantis, the right-wing governor of Florida, passed a measure that 'bans local governments from requiring heat and water breaks for outdoor workers.' Florida is, of course, a state that experiences a great deal of hot weather and where 'construction and farming are huge industries.'[9]

Other climate impacts will create the need for action by workers and their unions to an ever-greater degree. Extreme weather, floods, and wildfires will produce levels of destruction and dislocation that will involve major job losses, and chronic impacts such as drought will have huge economic effects. It will be necessary to ensure that public services and social benefit systems are greatly expanded and improved so that the climate crisis doesn't lead to the social abandonment of displaced workers.

As the struggle for a just transition away from fossil fuels unfolds, the power of organised workers will be essential. It will be necessary to ensure that transition proceeds as rapidly as possible, and the strike weapon must be used to compel employers and governments to act. It will also be vital, however, to ensure that, as environmentally destructive industries are replaced, workers aren't simply discarded. It has been recently noted in the case of the UK, for example, that North Sea oil workers mustn't experience the same fate as the miners in the 1980s.[10]

The worsening climate crisis will require decisive community-based resistance as well, and this will require the forging of a deeply rooted solidarity for survival. Certainly, the self-organisation that emerges will involve co-operative and mutual support initiatives that must develop in the face of adversity. However, state resources to deal with damage and disruption will have to be demanded and won as a matter of priority.

The situation that is developing requires that comprehensive plans and measures be put in place to deal with extreme weather and the chronic effects of climate change. The UK's Climate

Change Committee (CCC) warned in May 2024 that the country is 'absolutely lacking' in climate adaptation measures, placing agriculture, supply chains, power systems, and public health at risk.[11] Emergency services must be adequate, plans to evacuate threatened areas must be in place, and degraded healthcare systems and other public services must be strengthened to deal with disasters and lingering climate effects.

The process of planning to deal with these worsening impacts can't be left to political leaders and unaccountable bureaucrats. Communities will have to develop vital demands around their safety and well-being and take decisive action to ensure that they are met. Emergency food supplies and distribution systems must be in place. An infrastructure of survival must be established, from public cooling centres during extreme heat, to places of safety that can be accessed in the case of storms and floods. Safety and survival can't be the exclusive preserve of those who have the money to buy these things.

Global South

The imperialist world order we live under is based on a division between wealthy exploiter countries and those that are poor and exploited. Climate change brings a new and terrible element of inequality and injustice to this situation. The populations of the Global South contribute little to the climate crisis, but they must endure its impacts to a vastly disproportionate degree.

Waseem Ahmad, chief executive of Islamic Relief Worldwide, has noted that 'as climate-related catastrophes increase, it is the poorest and most vulnerable people who bear the brunt of the suffering. They are the ones most likely to live in fragile homes and least likely to have savings to fall back on, or assets to sell, or any kind of "Plan B" when floods hit and crops and livestock are wiped out.'[12]

In 2022, Pakistan was hit by the worst flooding in living memory and vast portions of the country were directly impacted. It is estimated that 33 million people lost their homes, land or jobs. One year after the floods, 'researchers from Islamic Relief who talked to people in the flood-affected areas found 40% of the children they surveyed had stunted growth and 25% were underweight as families struggle[d] to access food and healthcare.'

Yet, the countries of the Global South are crushed by debt, which they largely owe to institutions and banks that are based in rich countries. Last December, it was reported that the world's poor countries were having to allocate 38% of government revenues to debt servicing, 54% in the case of African countries.[13] Pakistan's acute debt crisis has just been staved off with a $7 billion loan.[14] This will buy its government a bit of time, but, in return, the IMF will require more commitments to impose austerity measures on the impoverished population. The country's malnourished children will stay hungry so that bankers in the West can be paid off.

As the debt crisis continues to cause immense harm and suffering in the Global South, the most powerful countries haggle at international summits about establishing a modest international fund to respond to the needs of impoverished countries that are harmed by the impacts of climate change. A Loss and Damage Fund is in the works, but, measured up against the vast debt load imposed on 'developing' these countries, it is hopelessly inadequate.[15]

Clearly, the movement that we build in the face of climate change must be solidly rooted in the principle of international solidarity, and this must involve an uncompromising struggle against the exploitation and abandonment of the Global South. In place of 'debt relief', we need the full repudiation of debt. The needs of poor people across the world are of much greater importance than the claims of parasitic lending institutions. When storms, floods, and drought cause destruction and dislocation, the resources needed to survive and rebuild must be available on a scale that far exceeds present token gestures.

The UN refugee agency estimates that, between 2008 and 2016, '21.5 million people were forcibly displaced each year by weather-related events.' It also suggests that 1.2 billion people 'could be displaced globally by 2050 due to climate change and natural disasters.'[16] Already, we see racist border enforcement and other methods being employed to try and exclude those driven by poverty and destabilisation to seek safety in Western countries. The years ahead will see millions of 'climate refugees' struggling for survival in this way, as portions of the earth become effectively uninhabitable. In such a catastrophic situation, the response to this forced movement of people must be just and viable on an international scale.

It becomes clearer with every passing month that the class struggle is being reshaped by the climate crisis. Capitalism's inability to create a sustainable relationship with the natural world is having devastating and rapidly worsening consequences for the bulk of humanity. Left to their own devices, those with economic and political power won't address the factors that are driving the crisis, or deal properly with the now inevitable climate impacts. The class struggle that we take up must be based on an active solidarity for survival and the goal of a rational and just society. In the face of the existential crisis that we are now confronting, there is simply no other way forward.

REFERENCES

1. Foster, John Bellamy (2022) *Capitalism in the Anthropocene: Ecological Ruin or Ecological Revolution*, New York: Monthly Review Press, p75
2. theguardian.com/environment/article/2024/jun/20/fossil-fuel-use-reaches-global-record-despite-clean-energy-growth
3. thenextrecession.wordpress.com/2024/06/23/fixing-the-climate-it-just-aint-profitable
4. Foster, p78
5. aljazeera.com/opinions/2023/12/19/there-is-a-way-out-of-the-climate-crisis-but-it-is-not-through-cop
6. cbc.ca/news/canada/windsor/migrant-workers-heat-1.7260417

7. fastcompany.com/91154102/working-in-gig-economy-during-extreme-heat-new-york

8. ilo.org/resource/news/climate-change-creates-cocktail-serious-health-hazards-70-cent-worlds

9. fox13news.com/news/desantis-signs-bill-banning-florida-counties-from-requiring-heat-and-water-breaks-for-outdoor-workers

10. theguardian.com/environment/article/2024/jul/01/north-sea-oil-transition-plan

11. edie.net/we-are-not-ready-at-all-poor-uk-climate-adaptation-policy-sparks-national-security-concerns

12. theguardian.com/global-development/2023/aug/05/a-year-on-the-devastating-long-term-effects-of-pakistans-floods-are-revealed

13. brettonwoodsproject.org/2023/12/new-data-show-global-south-is-in-worst-debt-crisis-ever-with-another-lost-decade-looming

14. imf.org/en/News/Articles/2024/07/12/pr-24273-pakistan-imf-reaches-agreement-on-economic-policies-for-37-month-eff

15. americas.iom.int/en/news/loss-and-damage-fund-operationalized-cop28

16. zurich.com/media/magazine/2022/there-could-be-1-2-billion-climate-refugees-by-2050-here-s-what-you-need-to-know

"Even an entire
society, a nation,
or all simultaneously
existing societies taken
together, are not owners of
the earth. They are simply
its possessors, its
beneficiaries, and... must
hand it down to succeeding
generations in an improved
condition"

Karl Marx

ABOUT THE AUTHORS

SARAH GLYNN is a writer and activist. She has worked as an architect in England and as a university lecturer in Scotland, and has researched issues around lower-income housing and around multiculturalism. She is now based in Strasbourg, where she works for the Kurdish Freedom Movement and writes a weekly column on Kurdish news.

Sarah played a central role in the establishment and running of the Scottish Unemployed Workers' Network (SUWN), which combined grassroots support with campaigning. She has also organised tenants' campaigns – especially against demolitions – and contributed to debates on housing policy. She was a housing activist before she was a housing academic, and the academic research fed into the activism. She has been active in campaigns for Palestinian rights and for Scottish independence.

Sarah is author or author/editor of: **Righting Welfare Wrongs: Dispatches and Analyses from the Front Line of the Fight against Austerity** (for the SUWN, Glasgow: Common Print 2016), **Byker: Newcastle upon Tyne** (Canterbury: Categorical Books 2015),

Class, Ethnicity and Religion: A political history of the Bengali East End (Manchester University Press 2014), and **Where the other half lives: lower-income housing in a neoliberal world** (London: Pluto Press 2009). She has also published many articles, both academic and popular, which you can find on her website: **sarahglynn.net**

JOHN CLARKE came to Canada from Britain in the late 1970s and settled in London, Ontario, where he became active in trade union struggles. In the early 80s, he helped to form a union of unemployed workers that forged links with similar organisations in other cities and challenged the grossly inadequate social benefits system in Ontario.

In 1990, the Ontario Coalition Against Poverty (OCAP) was formed and John moved to Toronto to become one of its organisers. He stayed in this role for 28 years, helping to mobilise poor communities that were facing a deepening austerity agenda at the hands of governments at every level.

In 2018, John was offered the position of Packer Visitor in Social Justice at Toronto's York University. There he developed and taught courses that related to the struggles of unions and social movements. He is presently teaching a course for union and community activists that considers the strategies those in power use to contain and control movements of social resistance, and how these can be overcome.

John remains active in anti-poverty struggles and is part of an organisation called 230 Fightback, which is resisting gentrification and fighting for social housing in Toronto's Downtown East. He also writes regularly for various publications on a range of issues related to working class resistance and popular struggles.

He can be reached at **clarkecourse@gmail.com**.